CONFESSING THE HEBREW SCRIPTURES

Adonai Hoo Sha•lom –

יְהוָה הוּא שָׁלוֹם

"THE LORD IS PEACE"

Confessing the Hebrew Scriptures
Adonai Hoo Shalom – The Lord Is Peace

Published by Jewish Voice Ministries International
PO Box 31998
Phoenix, AZ 85046-1998

Printed in China

ISBN 978-0-9821117-6-5

Confessing the Hebrew Scriptures

Adonai Hoo Sha•lom –

יְהוָה הוּא שָׁלוֹם

"THE LORD IS PEACE"

Jonathan Bernis

Introduction from Jonathan Bernis

The Power of Confession

It is my hope and prayer that this workbook, Volume 2 in my ***Confessing the Hebrew Scriptures*** series, will prove to be a rich blessing to your life. Over my 30+ years in ministry I have seen the fruit of confession of the Word of God. Through the process of confessing and hearing the Word, I have seen many healed, delivered and transformed. Proverbs 18:21 declares, "*death and life are in the power of the tongue.*" Our confession can bring either blessings or curses upon us and those we love. It is God's desire that we use our tongues to produce blessing, life, and faith according to His Word. So how do we accomplish this? How do we incorporate this biblical truth to work in our lives? The biblical principle is so very simple:

> *"So then faith cometh by hearing, and hearing by the word of God."* —Romans 10:17 KJV

From this verse, we understand that faith is built in us as we hear the Word of God. Notice, though, that hearing is mentioned twice. I believe this is because there are two kinds of hearing: hearing with our natural ears and hearing with the ears of our spirit. This is the process by which faith is deposited and released in our lives. We hear the Word of God as it is read and confessed, and over time, as we hear God's promises over and over again, it eventually drops down into our spirit, where our faith is then activated. When this incredible process happens, the promises of God become a reality in our life. This simple truth is what brings us into the reality of the salvation experience:

> ***"****For with the heart man believeth unto righteousness; and with the mouth confession is made unto salvation."* —Romans 10:10 KJV

This is what ***biblical*** confession is all about. It's about getting HIS Word… (which incidentally is His will) into our hearts, into our spirits. That's where faith must dwell in order to be activated—not the mind. Not only do we experience God's provision of salvation in this manner, but also all of the other promises given to us in Scripture are based on the same principle of "believing with the heart and confessing unto." The blessings God has provided for us in His Word, such as healing and health, deliverance, divine provision, and supernatural peace and comfort are all realized in exactly the same way. Every promise and blessing of God is acquired through faith. *But without faith, it is impossible to please Him* (Hebrews 11:6).

When God called Joshua to lead the Children of Israel into the Promised Land after the death of Moses, He gave him the following instructions:

Only be strong and very courageous, that you may observe to do according to all the law which Moses My servant commanded you; do not turn from it to the right hand or to the left, that you may prosper wherever you go. This Book of the Law shall not depart from your mouth, but you shall meditate in it day and night, that you may observe to do according to all that is written in it. For then you will make your way prosperous, and then you will have good success. —Joshua 1:7-8

While the Christian concept of meditation is derived from the Latin word "to consider or contemplate" and has more to do with reflection—the process of deliberately focusing on specific Scriptures and reflecting on their meaning—the Hebrew has two concepts or a "dual concept" of meditation. The first, שיחה, *(seecha)* has to do with rehearing in one's mind or thoughts and is similar to the Christian concept of meditation. The other, הגה (*hagah)* is not reflection with the *mind*, but with the *mouth*—to rehearse the Word of God in speech, "to speak, talk, utter, or mutter." This is the Hebrew word used in the above text. It is this concept and practice of meditation that the Lord tells Joshua will make him both "*prosperous and successful.*"

It stands to reason that if God told Joshua that confession of His Word would make him prosperous and successful, then we also can experience the same prosperity and success he experienced if we follow the same principles.

The Significance of Hebrew

While most of us understand that the Old Testament Scriptures were written primarily in the Hebrew language, very few of us can actually read or understand Hebrew. Therefore, we are forced to read the various English translations of the Bible. And while there are many excellent translations out there, they often miss the nuances, insight, and deeper revelation found in the original Hebrew.

For example, God reveals Himself through different Hebrew names in the Tanakh (Old Testament). Names such as El Shaddai *God Almighty*, Adonai-Yereh *The LORD our Provider*, Adonai-Tzidkaynu *The LORD our Righteousness*, Adonai-Nissi *The LORD our Banner*, Adonai- Rofecha *The LORD our Healer* (see my previous workbook on this one), and now Adonai-Shalom *The LORD our Peace*, reveal His character, His attributes, His very nature. When we dig into these names in the Hebrew, we gain extraordinary insight into who the LORD is and what He has provided for us. The benefits promised to us in the Bible, promises of healing and health, salvation, deliverance, divine provision, supernatural peace, and so on are all originally in Hebrew.

So, while there is no doubt that because the LORD is omniscient, He responds to any language and that confession of the Word of God in any language is going to release power and blessing. If we want to experience the greatest impact, the greatest depth, and the fullest meaning, we must go back to the roots. And those roots are Hebrew. The ancient Hebrew sages taught that although it was permissible to pray in other languages, praying in *Lashon HaKodesh*, the Holy Tongue, was always preferable, even if the person did not understand the words.

How to Use the Workbook and CD

You may be saying to yourself at this point, "This is all well and good, but how can I do this?" How is this possible—to confess the Scriptures in the original Hebrew without going to Bible school or seminary, without undertaking an extensive study of Hebrew? The good news is there is a way. The answer is found in a system developed by the Reform Movement of American Judaism.

As Jews immigrated to America in the late 19th and early part of the 20th century from the *"Old Country"* of Eastern and Central Europe to forge a new life free from the bitter anti-Semitism they had endured for so long, they quickly began to assimilate into American culture. Hebrew education, which was a mandatory part of their former prayer life (as well as Yiddish as a spoken language) began to disappear. In order to preserve Hebrew prayer in their synagogues, a method called *transliteration* was employed. This simple process, which we see utilized in dictionaries, uses English letters to sound out the Hebrew words. In other words, the Hebrew text is converted to English in order to read and pronounce the original Hebrew.

Let's look at a few examples to understand how this works:

- The Hebrew word for "peace" is שָׁלוֹם , *Shalom.* While you may recognize this Hebrew word from seeing it often enough (and, of course, you will see it a lot in this volume since that is the divine Name we are focusing on here), most cannot read the actual Hebrew characters. But when we use the transliteration method, it now becomes very readable: **sha•lome**
- Let's try another one. The Hebrew word for *Jerusalem is* יְרוּשָׁלַיִם . While few can read the actual Hebrew, when we apply the transliteration method, it becomes easy: **Ye•roo•sha•la•yim**
- One last example is a bit more challenging. Many Jewish prayers begin this way: *"Blessed are you, O Lord our God, King of the Universe"* in Hebrew:

בָּרוּךְ אַתָּה יְיָ אֱלֹהֵינוּ מֶלֶךְ הָעוֹלָם

Even more complex sentences such as these become easy to recite with the transliteration method and a bit of practice:

Ba•ruch a•tah Ado•nai Elo•hei•nu Me•lech Ha•o•lam

And off you go. It's that easy. No seminary training, no intensive Hebrew study. Just begin to work through the pages using this simple yet effective transliteration method and you will be confessing the Scriptures in the ancient Hebrew tongue! Each page has a Scripture promise relating to Adonai (the word used by the Jewish community in substitution for the Hebrew name translated LORD, the Tetragrammaton, often pronounced *Jehovah* or *Yaweh*) Shalom: *The Lord Is Peace* and contains the text in Hebrew, English, and English Transliteration directly from the Hebrew.

We have painstakingly worked to make sure the Hebrew text is completely accurate, and I have selected Scriptures that bring out what I feel are the most complete meaning of ***shalom***, which although translated most often *peace*, also means *wholeness, welfare, rest, safety, wellbeing, prosperity, success, health, completeness,* and *fullness*. The root verb is best translated: *"to bring to completion."* Thus, when we are exhorted in Psalm 122:6 to *"pray for the peace (**shalom**) of Jerusalem,"* we are literally to pray for God to bring to completion His plan and purpose for the Land and People of Jerusalem.

Along with the workbook, we've included a companion CD so you can hear how each Scripture sounds when spoken by a native Israeli Hebrew speaker. I suggest you begin by playing the CD and following along in the English and transliterated Hebrew from Scripture to Scripture. After, try confessing the Hebrew transliteration along with the CD to learn which syllables to accent. In no time, you will be confessing these Scriptures in Hebrew just like a native-born Israeli. It really is that easy!

Finally, let me share with you four things to keep in mind as you put these Hebrew prayers to work for God to bring peace into your life:

1. **Let the Scriptures fill your heart.** As you pray and confess these powerful promises of God, ask Him to make the Word come alive in your life. Watch as your faith grows on a daily basis!
2. **Be confident in the goodness of God.** Since these prayers are taken directly from the Hebrew Scriptures, you can know that you are praying perfectly in line with God's will for your life.
3. **Confession is a simple act of trust and obedience.** This is not some mysterious, mystical act. It is simply believing and acting on the truth of God's Word. As you are diligent to exercise this powerful principle in your life day by day, you will be amazed as you watch it take hold in your life and result in transformation.
4. **Know that God's promises are true.** I encourage you to confess these promises of healing and health boldly and with expectation that you and your loved ones will experience exactly what God promises He will do. Remember, God is the same yesterday, today, and forever.

You may wish to read through the entire book at one sitting. You may choose to take one prayer in order each day during your personal time with God. You may find specific Scriptures are particularly meaningful in your specific situation and want to listen to them again and again. No matter how you utilize this workbook, I have no doubt that if you exercise this powerful principle of confessing God's Word in your daily devotions, it **will** bear fruit. You **will** be changed…

"So shall My word be that goes forth from My mouth; It shall not return to Me void, But it shall accomplish what I please, And it shall prosper in the thing for which I sent it." —Isaiah 55:11

Jonathan Bernis, Phoenix, Arizona

CONFESSING THE HEBREW SCRIPTURES

Adonai Hoo Sha•lom – יְהוָה הוּא שָׁלוֹם

"THE LORD IS PEACE"

The Lord bless you and keep you; The Lord make His face shine upon you, And be gracious to you; The Lord lift up His countenance upon you, And give you peace.

Numbers 6:24-26

יְבָרֶכְךָ יְהוָה וְיִשְׁמְרֶךָ׃
יָאֵר יְהוָה פָּנָיו אֵלֶיךָ וִיחֻנֶּךָּ׃
יִשָּׂא יְהוָה פָּנָיו אֵלֶיךָ וְיָשֵׂם לְךָ שָׁלוֹם׃

Ye•va•re•che•chá Adonái ve•yish•me•ré•cha.
Ya•ér Adonái pa•nav e•lé•cha viy•chu•né•ka.
Yi•sa Adonái pa•nav e•lé•cha ve•yá•sem le•chá sha•lom.

Confessing the Hebrew Scriptures

Adonai Hoo Sha•lom – יְהוָה הוּא שָׁלוֹם

"THE LORD IS PEACE"

The eternal God is your refuge, And underneath are the everlasting arms; He will thrust out the enemy from before you, And will say, 'Destroy!'

Deuteronomy 33:27

מְעֹנָה אֱלֹהֵי קֶדֶם וּמִתַּחַת זְרֹעֹת עוֹלָם וַיְגָרֶשׁ מִפָּנֶיךָ אוֹיֵב וַיֹּאמֶר הַשְׁמֵד:

Me•o•na Elo•hey ké•dem oo•mi•tá•chat ze•ro•ot o•lam va•ye•gá•resh mi•pa•né•cha o•yev va•yó•mer hash•med.

Then the Lord said to him, "Peace be with you; do not fear, you shall not die." So Gideon built an altar there to the Lord, and called it The-Lord-Is-Peace...

Judges 6:23-24

וַיֹּאמֶר לוֹ יְהוָה שָׁלוֹם לְךָ אַל-תִּירָא לֹא תָּמוּת:
וַיִּבֶן שָׁם גִּדְעוֹן מִזְבֵּחַ לַיהוָה וַיִּקְרָא-לוֹ יְהוָה שָׁלוֹם

Va•yó•mer lo Adonái sha•lom le•chá al-ti•ra lo ta•moot.
Va•yí•ven sham Gid•ón miz•bé•ach la•Adonái va•yik•ra-lo Adonái Sha•lom.

Confessing the Hebrew Scriptures

Adonai Hoo Sha•lom – יְהוָה הוּא שָׁלוֹם

"THE LORD IS PEACE"

And thus you shall say to him who lives in prosperity: "Peace be to you, peace to your house, and peace to all that you have!"

I Samuel 25:6

וַאֲמַרְתֶּם כֹּה לֶחָי וְאַתָּה שָׁלוֹם וּבֵיתְךָ שָׁלוֹם וְכֹל אֲשֶׁר-לְךָ שָׁלוֹם׃

Va•amar•tem ko le•chái ve•ata sha•lom oo•veyt•cha sha•lom ve•chol ashér-le•chá sha•lom.

I will both lie down in peace, and sleep; For You alone, O Lord, make me dwell in safety.

Psalm 4:8

בְּשָׁלוֹם יַחְדָּו אֶשְׁכְּבָה וְאִישָׁן כִּי-אַתָּה יְהוָה לְבָדָד לָבֶטַח תּוֹשִׁיבֵנִי׃

Be•sha•lom yach•dav esh•ke•va ve•ee•shan ki-ata Adonái le•va•dad la•vé•tach to•shi•véni.

Adonai Hoo Sha•lom – יְהוָה הוּא שָׁלוֹם

"THE LORD IS PEACE"

The Lord is my rock and my fortress and my deliverer; My God, my strength, in whom I will trust; My shield and the horn of my salvation, my stronghold.

Psalm 18:2

יְהוָה סַלְעִי וּמְצוּדָתִי וּמְפַלְטִי אֵלִי צוּרִי אֶחֱסֶה-בּוֹ מָגִנִּי וְקֶרֶן יִשְׁעִי מִשְׂגַּבִּי:

Adonái sal•ée oo•me•tzu•da•ti oo•me•fal•ti Elí tzu•ri e•ch•esé-bo ma•gi•ni ve•ké•ren yish•ée mis•ga•bi.

Confessing the Hebrew Scriptures

Adonai Hoo Sha•lom – יְהוָה הוּא שָׁלוֹם

"THE LORD IS PEACE"

...the Lord is my shepherd; I shall not want. He makes me to lie down in green pastures; He leads me beside the still waters. He restores my soul; He leads me in the paths of righteousness For His name's sake. Yea, though I walk through the valley of the shadow of death, I will fear no evil; For You are with me; Your rod and Your staff, they comfort me. You prepare a table before me in the presence of my enemies; You anoint my head with oil; My cup runs over. Surely goodness and mercy shall follow me all the days of my life; And I will dwell in the house of the Lord Forever. Psalm 23

... יְהוָה רֹעִי לֹא אֶחְסָר:
בִּנְאוֹת דֶּשֶׁא יַרְבִּיצֵנִי עַל-מֵי מְנֻחוֹת יְנַהֲלֵנִי:
נַפְשִׁי יְשׁוֹבֵב יַנְחֵנִי בְמַעְגְּלֵי-צֶדֶק לְמַעַן שְׁמוֹ:
גַּם כִּי-אֵלֵךְ בְּגֵיא צַלְמָוֶת לֹא-אִירָא רָע כִּי-אַתָּה עִמָּדִי שִׁבְטְךָ וּמִשְׁעַנְתֶּךָ
הֵמָּה יְנַחֲמֻנִי:
תַּעֲרֹךְ לְפָנַי שֻׁלְחָן נֶגֶד צֹרְרָי דִּשַּׁנְתָּ בַשֶּׁמֶן רֹאשִׁי כּוֹסִי רְוָיָה:
אַךְ טוֹב וָחֶסֶד יִרְדְּפוּנִי כָּל-יְמֵי חַיָּי וְשַׁבְתִּי בְּבֵית-יְהוָה לְאֹרֶךְ יָמִים:

... Adonái ro•ée lo ech•sar.
Bin•ót dé•she yar•bi•tzé•ni al-méy me•nu•chót ye•na•ha•lé•ni.
Naf•shí ye•sho•vév yan•ché•ni ve•ma•ag•léy-tzé•dek le•má•an sh'mo.
Gam ki-e•léch be•géy tzal•má•vet lo-ee•rá ra ki-ata ee•ma•di shiv•te•chá oo•mish•an•té•cha hé•ma ye•na•cha•mú•ni.
Ta•a•róch le•fa•nái shool•chan né•ged tzo•re•rái di•shán•ta va•shé•men ro•shí ko•sí re•va•yá.
Ach tov va•ché•sed yir•de•fú•ni kol-ye•méy cha•yay ve•sháv•ti be•veyt-Adonái le•ó•rech ya•mim.

CONFESSING THE HEBREW SCRIPTURES

Adonai Hoo Sha•lom – יְהוָה הוּא שָׁלוֹם

"THE LORD IS PEACE"

...the Lord is my light and my salvation; Whom shall I fear? The Lord is the strength of my life; of whom shall I be afraid?

Psalm 27:1

... יְהוָה אוֹרִי וְיִשְׁעִי מִמִּי אִירָא יְהוָה מָעוֹז חַיַּי מִמִּי אֶפְחָד:

... Adonái o•ri ve•yish•ée mi•mi ee•ra Adonái ma•oz cha•yái mi•mi ef•chad.

The Lord is my strength and my shield; My heart trusted in Him, and I am helped; Therefore my heart greatly rejoices, and with my song I will praise Him.

Psalm 28:7

יְהוָה עֻזִּי וּמָגִנִּי בּוֹ בָטַח לִבִּי וְנֶעֱזָרְתִּי וַיַּעֲלֹז לִבִּי וּמִשִּׁירִי אֲהוֹדֶנּוּ:

Adonái oo•zi oo•ma•gi•ni bo va•tach li•bi ve•ne•ezár•ti va•ya•a•loz li•bi oo•mi•shi•ri aho•dé•nu.

CONFESSING THE HEBREW SCRIPTURES

Adonai Hoo Sha•lom – יְהוָה הוּא שָׁלוֹם

"THE LORD IS PEACE"

The Lord will give strength to His people; The Lord will bless His people with peace.

Psalm 29:11

יְהוָה עֹז לְעַמּוֹ יִתֵּן יְהוָה יְבָרֵךְ אֶת-עַמּוֹ בַשָּׁלוֹם׃

Adonái oz le•a•mo yi•ten Adonái ye•va•rech et-amo va•sha•lom.

You are my hiding place; You shall preserve me from trouble; You shall surround me with songs of deliverance. Selah.

Psalm 32:7

אַתָּה סֵתֶר לִי מִצַּר תִּצְּרֵנִי רָנֵּי פַלֵּט תְּסוֹבְבֵנִי סֶלָה׃

Ata sé•ter li mi•tzar titz•ré•ni ro•néy fa•let te•so•ve•véni Séla.

Confessing the Hebrew Scriptures

Adonai Hoo Sha•lom – יְהוָה הוּא שָׁלוֹם

"THE LORD IS PEACE"

God is our refuge and strength, a very present help in trouble.

Psalm 46:1

אֱלֹהִים לָנוּ מַחֲסֶה וָעֹז עֶזְרָה בְצָרוֹת נִמְצָא מְאֹד׃

Elohím lá•nu ma•cha•sé va•oz ez•ra ve•tza•rot nim•tza me•od.

He has redeemed my soul in peace from the battle that was against me...

Psalm 55:18

פָּדָה בְשָׁלוֹם נַפְשִׁי מִקְּרָב-לִי כִּי-בְרַבִּים הָיוּ עִמָּדִי׃

Pa•da ve•sha•lom naf•shi mik•rav-li ki-ve•ra•bim ha•yu ee•ma•di.

Adonai Hoo Sha•lom – יְהוָה הוּא שָׁלוֹם

"THE LORD IS PEACE"

From the end of the earth I will cry to You, when my heart is overwhelmed; Lead me to the rock that is higher than I. For You have been a shelter for me, a strong tower from the enemy. I will abide in Your tabernacle forever; I will trust in the shelter of Your wings...

Psalm 61:2-4

מִקְצֵה הָאָרֶץ אֵלֶיךָ אֶקְרָא בַּעֲטֹף לִבִּי בְּצוּר-יָרוּם מִמֶּנִּי תַנְחֵנִי:
כִּי-הָיִיתָ מַחְסֶה לִי מִגְדַּל-עֹז מִפְּנֵי אוֹיֵב:
אָגוּרָה בְאָהָלְךָ עוֹלָמִים אֶחֱסֶה בְסֵתֶר כְּנָפֶיךָ ...:

Mik•tzé ha•á•retz e•lé•cha ek•ra ba•a•tof li•bi be•tzur-ya•room mi•mé•ni tan•ché•ni.
Ki-ha•yí•ta mach•sé li mig•dal-oz mip•néy o•yev.
Agú•ra ve•o•hol•cha o•la•mim e•che•sé ve•sé•ter ke•na•fé•cha ...

Adonai Hoo Sha•lom – יְהוָה הוּא שָׁלוֹם

"THE LORD IS PEACE"

He shall come down like rain upon the grass before mowing, like showers that water the earth. In His days the righteous shall flourish, and abundance of peace, until the moon is no more.

Psalm 72:6-7

יֵרֵד כְּמָטָר עַל-גֵּז כִּרְבִיבִים זַרְזִיף אָרֶץ:
יִפְרַח בְּיָמָיו צַדִּיק וְרֹב שָׁלוֹם עַד-בְּלִי יָרֵחַ:

Ye•red ke•ma•tar al-gez kir•vi•vim zar•zif á•retz.
Yif•rach be•ya•mav tza•dik ve•rov sha•lom ad-be•li ya•ré•ach.

But it is good for me to draw near to God; I have put my trust in the Lord GOD, That I may declare all Your works.

Psalm 73:28

וַאֲנִי קִרֲבַת אֱלֹהִים לִי טוֹב שַׁתִּי בַּאדֹנָי יֱהוִֹה מַחְסִי לְסַפֵּר כָּל-מַלְאֲכוֹתֶיךָ:

Va•ani kir•vat Elohím li tov sha•tí ba•Adonái Elohím mach•si le•sa•per kol-mal•a•cho•té•cha.

Confessing the Hebrew Scriptures

Adonai Hoo Sha•lom – יְהוָה הוּא שָׁלוֹם

"THE LORD IS PEACE"

I will hear what God the Lord will speak, For He will speak peace To His people and to His saints...

Psalm 85:8

אֶשְׁמְעָה מַה-יְדַבֵּר הָאֵל יְהוָה כִּי-יְדַבֵּר שָׁלוֹם אֶל-עַמּוֹ וְאֶל-חֲסִידָיו ...

Esh•me•áh ma-ye•da•ber ha•El Adonái ki-ye•da•ber sha•lom el-amo ve•el-cha•si•dav ...

He who dwells in the secret place of the Most High shall abide under the shadow of the Almighty. I will say of the Lord, "He is my refuge and my fortress; My God, in Him I will trust."

Psalm 91:1-2

יֹשֵׁב בְּסֵתֶר עֶלְיוֹן בְּצֵל שַׁדַּי יִתְלוֹנָן:
אֹמַר לַיהוָה מַחְסִי וּמְצוּדָתִי אֱלֹהַי אֶבְטַח-בּוֹ:

Yo•shev be•sé•ter Elyon be•tzel Sha•dái yit•lo•nan.
Omar la•Adonái mach•si oo•me•tzu•da•ti Elo•hái ev•tach-bo.

CONFESSING THE HEBREW SCRIPTURES

Adonai Hoo Sha•lom – יְהוָה הוּא שָׁלוֹם

"THE LORD IS PEACE"

Because he has set his love upon Me, therefore I will deliver him; I will set him on high, because he has known My name. He shall call upon Me, and I will answer him; I will be with him in trouble; I will deliver him and honor him. With long life I will satisfy him, and show him My salvation.

Psalm 91:14-16

כִּי בִי חָשַׁק וַאֲפַלְּטֵהוּ אֲשַׂגְּבֵהוּ כִּי-יָדַע שְׁמִי:
יִקְרָאֵנִי וְאֶעֱנֵהוּ עִמּוֹ-אָנֹכִי בְצָרָה אֲחַלְּצֵהוּ וַאֲכַבְּדֵהוּ:
אֹרֶךְ יָמִים אַשְׂבִּיעֵהוּ וְאַרְאֵהוּ בִּישׁוּעָתִי:

Ki vi cha•shak va•a•fal•té•hu asag•vé•hu ki-ya•da sh'mi.
Yik•ra•éni ve•e•ené•hu ee•mo-Ano•chi ve•tza•ra a•chal•tzé•hu va•a•chab•dé•hu.
Ó•rech ya•mim as•bi•é•hu ve•ar•é•hu bi•ye•shu•ati.

CONFESSING THE HEBREW SCRIPTURES

Adonai Hoo Sha•lom – יְהוָה הוּא שָׁלוֹם

"THE LORD IS PEACE"

Great peace have those who love Your law, and nothing causes them to stumble.

Psalm 119:165

שָׁלוֹם רָב לְאֹהֲבֵי תוֹרָתֶךָ וְאֵין לָמוֹ מִכְשׁוֹל:

Sha•lom rav le•oha•véy Tora•té•cha ve•eyn lá•mo mich•shol.

Confessing the Hebrew Scriptures

Adonai Hoo Sha•lom – יְהוָה הוּא שָׁלוֹם

"THE LORD IS PEACE"

...I will lift up my eyes to the hills—from whence comes my help? My help comes from the Lord, Who made heaven and earth. He will not allow your foot to be moved; He who keeps you will not slumber. Behold, He who keeps Israel shall neither slumber nor sleep. The Lord is your keeper; The Lord is your shade at your right hand. The sun shall not strike you by day, nor the moon by night. The Lord shall preserve you from all evil; He shall preserve your soul. The Lord shall preserve your going out and your coming in from this time forth, and even forevermore. Psalm 121

... אֶשָּׂא עֵינַי אֶל-הֶהָרִים מֵאַיִן יָבֹא עֶזְרִי:
עֶזְרִי מֵעִם יְהוָה עֹשֵׂה שָׁמַיִם וָאָרֶץ:
אַל-יִתֵּן לַמּוֹט רַגְלֶךָ אַל-יָנוּם שֹׁמְרֶךָ:
הִנֵּה לֹא יָנוּם וְלֹא יִישָׁן שׁוֹמֵר יִשְׂרָאֵל:
יְהוָה שֹׁמְרֶךָ יְהוָה צִלְּךָ עַל-יַד יְמִינֶךָ:
יוֹמָם הַשֶּׁמֶשׁ לֹא-יַכֶּכָּה וְיָרֵחַ בַּלָּיְלָה:
יְהוָה יִשְׁמָרְךָ מִכָּל-רָע יִשְׁמֹר אֶת-נַפְשֶׁךָ:
יְהוָה יִשְׁמָר-צֵאתְךָ וּבוֹאֶךָ מֵעַתָּה וְעַד-עוֹלָם:

... esa ey•nái el-he•ha•rim me•á•yin ya•vo ez•ri.
Ez•ri me•eem Adonái o•sé sha•má•yim va•á•retz.
Al-yi•ten la•mot rag•lé•cha al - ya•noom shom•ré•cha.
Hi•né lo ya•noom ve•lo yi•shan sho•mer Israél.
Adonái shom•ré•cha Adonái tzil•cha al-yad ye•mi•né•cha.
Yo•mam ha•shé•mesh lo-ya•kéka ve•ya•ré•ach ba•lái•la.
Adonái yish•mor•cha mi•kol-ra yish•mor et - naf•shé•cha.
Adonái yish•mor-tzet•cha oo•vo•é•cha me•ata ve•ad-o•lam.

Confessing the Hebrew Scriptures

Adonai Hoo Sha•lom – יְהוָה הוּא שָׁלוֹם

"THE LORD IS PEACE"

Pray for the peace of Jerusalem: "May they prosper who love you. Peace be within your walls, prosperity within your palaces." For the sake of my brethren and companions, I will now say, "Peace be within you." Because of the house of the Lord our God I will seek your good.

Psalm 122:6-9

שַׁאֲלוּ שְׁלוֹם יְרוּשָׁלָם יִשְׁלָיוּ אֹהֲבָיִךְ׃
יְהִי־שָׁלוֹם בְּחֵילֵךְ שַׁלְוָה בְּאַרְמְנוֹתָיִךְ׃
לְמַעַן־אַחַי וְרֵעָי אֲדַבְּרָה־נָּא שָׁלוֹם בָּךְ׃
לְמַעַן בֵּית־יְהוָה אֱלֹהֵינוּ אֲבַקְשָׁה טוֹב לָךְ׃

Sha•a•lú sh'lom Yeru•sha•láyim yish•lá•yu o•ha•vá•yich.
Ye•hi-sha•lom be•chey•léch shal•va be•ar•me•no•tá•yich.
Le•má•an-a•chái ve•re•ái adab•ra-na sha•lom bach.
Le•má•an beyt-Adonái Elo•héy•nu avak•sha tov lach.

Adonai Hoo Sha•lom – יְהוָה הוּא שָׁלוֹם

"THE LORD IS PEACE"

...Those who trust in the Lord are like Mount Zion, which cannot be moved, but abides forever. As the mountains surround Jerusalem, so the Lord surrounds His people from this time forth and forever.

Psalm 125:1-2

...הַבֹּטְחִים בַּיהוָה כְּהַר-צִיּוֹן לֹא-יִמּוֹט לְעוֹלָם יֵשֵׁב:
יְרוּשָׁלַםִ הָרִים סָבִיב לָהּ וַיהוָה סָבִיב לְעַמּוֹ מֵעַתָּה וְעַד-עוֹלָם:

... ha•bot•chim ba•Adonái ke•Har-Tzi•yon lo-yi•mot le•o•lam ye•shev. Yeru•sha•láyim ha•rim sa•viv láh va•Adonái sa•viv le•a•mo me•ata ve•ad-o•lam.

Confessing the Hebrew Scriptures

Adonai Hoo Sha•lom – יְהוָה הוּא שָׁלוֹם

"THE LORD IS PEACE"

Behold, God is my salvation, I will trust and not be afraid; 'For Yah, the Lord, is my strength and song; He also has become my salvation.'

Isaiah 12:2

הִנֵּה אֵל יְשׁוּעָתִי אֶבְטַח וְלֹא אֶפְחָד כִּי עָזִּי וְזִמְרָת יָהּ יְהוָה וַיְהִי-לִי לִישׁוּעָה׃

Hi•né El ye•shu•ati ev•tach ve•lo ef•chad ki ozi ve•zim•rat Yah Adonái va•ye•hi-li li•ye•shu•áh.

You will keep him in perfect peace, whose mind is stayed on You, because he trusts in You.

Isaiah 26:3

יֵצֶר סָמוּךְ תִּצֹּר שָׁלוֹם שָׁלוֹם כִּי בְךָ בָּטוּחַ׃

Yé•tzer sa•mooch ti•tzor sha•lom sha•lom ki ve•cha ba•tú•ach.

Adonai Hoo Sha•lom – יְהוָה הוּא שָׁלוֹם

"THE LORD IS PEACE"

The work of righteousness will be peace, and the effect of righteousness, quietness and assurance forever. My people will dwell in a peaceful habitation, in secure dwellings, and in quiet resting places.

Isaiah 32:17-18

וְהָיָה מַעֲשֵׂה הַצְּדָקָה שָׁלוֹם וַעֲבֹדַת הַצְּדָקָה הַשְׁקֵט וָבֶטַח עַד-עוֹלָם:
וְיָשַׁב עַמִּי בִּנְוֵה שָׁלוֹם וּבְמִשְׁכְּנוֹת מִבְטַחִים וּבִמְנוּחֹת שַׁאֲנַנּוֹת:

Ve•ha•ya ma•asé hatz•da•ká sha•lom va•avo•dat hatz•da•ká hash•ket va•vé•tach ad-o•lam.
Ve•ya•shav ami bin•vé sha•lom oo•ve•mish•ke•not miv•ta•chim oo•vim•nu•chot sha•ana•not.

CONFESSING THE HEBREW SCRIPTURES

Adonai Hoo Sha•lom – יְהוָה הוּא שָׁלוֹם

"THE LORD IS PEACE"

But those who wait on the Lord shall renew their strength; they shall mount up with wings like eagles, they shall run and not be weary, they shall walk and not faint.

Isaiah 40:31

וְקוֵֹי יְהוָה יַחֲלִיפוּ כֹחַ יַעֲלוּ אֵבֶר כַּנְּשָׁרִים יָרוּצוּ וְלֹא יִיגָעוּ יֵלְכוּ וְלֹא יִיעָפוּ׃

Ve•ko•véy Adonái ya•cha•lí•fu chó•ach ya•alu éver kan•sha•rim ya•rú•tzu ve•lo yi•gá•oo yel•chu ve•lo yiá•fu.

Fear not, for I am with you; Be not dismayed, for I am your God. I will strengthen you, yes, I will help you, I will uphold you with My righteous right hand.

Isaiah 41:10

אַל-תִּירָא כִּי עִמְּךָ-אָנִי אַל-תִּשְׁתָּע כִּי-אֲנִי אֱלֹהֶיךָ אִמַּצְתִּיךָ אַף-עֲזַרְתִּיךָ
אַף-תְּמַכְתִּיךָ בִּימִין צִדְקִי׃

Al-ti•ra ki eem•cha-Áni al-tish•ta ki-Ani Elo•hé•cha ee•matz•tí•cha af-azar•tí•cha af-te•mach•tí•cha bi•ye•min tzid•ki.

CONFESSING THE HEBREW SCRIPTURES

Adonai Hoo Sha•lom – יְהוָה הוּא שָׁלוֹם

"THE LORD IS PEACE"

...Fear not, for I have redeemed you; I have called you by your name; You are Mine. When you pass through the waters, I will be with you; And through the rivers, they shall not overflow you. When you walk through the fire, you shall not be burned, nor shall the flame scorch you.

Isaiah 43:1-2

אַל-תִּירָא כִּי גְאַלְתִּיךָ קָרָאתִי בְשִׁמְךָ לִי-אָתָּה:
כִּי-תַעֲבֹר בַּמַּיִם אִתְּךָ-אָנִי וּבַנְּהָרוֹת לֹא יִשְׁטְפוּךָ כִּי-תֵלֵךְ בְּמוֹ-אֵשׁ לֹא תִכָּוֶה
וְלֶהָבָה לֹא תִבְעַר-בָּךְ:

Al-ti•ra ki ge•al•tí•cha ka•rá•ti ve•shim•cha li-áta.
Ki-ta•a•vor ba•má•yim eet•cha-Áni oo•van•ha•rot lo yish•te•fú•cha ki-te•lech be•mo-esh lo ti•ka•vé ve•le•ha•va lo tiv•ar-bach.

CONFESSING THE HEBREW SCRIPTURES

Adonai Hoo Sha•lom – יְהוָה הוּא שָׁלוֹם

"THE LORD IS PEACE"

But He was wounded for our transgressions, He was bruised for our iniquities; The chastisement for our peace was upon Him, and by His stripes we are healed.

Isaiah 53:5

וְהוּא מְחֹלָל מִפְּשָׁעֵנוּ מְדֻכָּא מֵעֲוֺנֹתֵינוּ מוּסַר שְׁלוֹמֵנוּ עָלָיו וּבַחֲבֻרָתוֹ
נִרְפָּא-לָנוּ:

Ve•hu me•cho•lal mip•sha•é•nu me•du•ka me•avo•no•téy•nu mu•sar sh'lo•mé•nu a•lav oo•va•cha•vu•ra•to nir•pa-lá•nu.

Confessing the Hebrew Scriptures

Adonai Hoo Sha•lom – יְהוָה הוּא שָׁלוֹם

"THE LORD IS PEACE"

For the mountains shall depart and the hills be removed, but My kindness shall not depart from you, nor shall My covenant of peace be removed," says the Lord, who has mercy on you.

Isaiah 54:10

כִּי הֶהָרִים יָמוּשׁוּ וְהַגְּבָעוֹת תְּמוּטֶינָה וְחַסְדִּי מֵאִתֵּךְ לֹא-יָמוּשׁ וּבְרִית שְׁלוֹמִי לֹא תָמוּט אָמַר מְרַחֲמֵךְ יְהוָה:

Ki he•ha•rim ya•mú•shu ve•hag•va•ot te•mu•téy•na ve•chas•di me•ee•tech lo-ya•moosh oo•ve•rit sh'lo•mi lo ta•moot amar me•ra•cha•mech Adonái.

All your children shall be taught by the Lord, and great shall be the peace of your children.

Isaiah 54:13

וְכָל-בָּנַיִךְ לִמּוּדֵי יְהוָה וְרַב שְׁלוֹם בָּנָיִךְ:

Ve•chol-ba•ná•yich li•mu•déy Adonái ve•rav sh'lom ba•ná•yich.

Confessing the Hebrew Scriptures

Adonai Hoo Sha•lom – יְהוָה הוּא שָׁלוֹם

"THE LORD IS PEACE"

For I know the thoughts that I think toward you, says the Lord, thoughts of peace and not of evil, to give you a future and a hope. Then you will call upon Me and go and pray to Me, and I will listen to you. And you will seek Me and find Me, when you search for Me with all your heart.

Jeremiah 29:11-13

כִּי אָנֹכִי יָדַעְתִּי אֶת-הַמַּחֲשָׁבֹת אֲשֶׁר אָנֹכִי חֹשֵׁב עֲלֵיכֶם נְאֻם-יְהוָה
מַחְשְׁבוֹת שָׁלוֹם וְלֹא לְרָעָה לָתֵת לָכֶם אַחֲרִית וְתִקְוָה:
וּקְרָאתֶם אֹתִי וַהֲלַכְתֶּם וְהִתְפַּלַּלְתֶּם אֵלָי וְשָׁמַעְתִּי אֲלֵיכֶם:
וּבִקַּשְׁתֶּם אֹתִי וּמְצָאתֶם כִּי תִדְרְשֻׁנִי בְּכָל-לְבַבְכֶם:

Ki Ano•chi ya•dá•ati et-ha•ma•cha•sha•vot ashér Ano•chi cho•shev a•ley•chem ne•oom-Adonái mach•she•vot sha•lom ve•lo le•ra•ah la•tet la•chém a•cha•rit ve•tik•va.
Ook•ra•tem o•ti va•ha•lach•tem ve•hit•pa•lal•tem e•lái ve•sha•má•ati a•ley•chem.
Oo•vi•kash•tem o•ti oo•me•tza•tem ki tid•re•shú•ni be•chol-le•vav•chem.

CONFESSING THE HEBREW SCRIPTURES

Adonai Hoo Sha•lom – יְהוָה הוּא שָׁלוֹם

"THE LORD IS PEACE"

..."O man greatly beloved, fear not! Peace be to you; be strong, yes, be strong!" So when he spoke to me I was strengthened, and said, "Let my lord speak, for you have strengthened me."

Daniel 10:19

... אַל-תִּירָא אִישׁ-חֲמֻדוֹת שָׁלוֹם לָךְ חֲזַק וַחֲזָק וּבְדַבְּרוֹ עִמִּי הִתְחַזַּקְתִּי וָאֹמְרָה יְדַבֵּר אֲדֹנִי כִּי חִזַּקְתָּנִי׃

... al-ti•ra eesh-cha•mu•dot sha•lom lach cha•zak va•cha•zak oo•ve•dab•ro ee•mi hit•cha•zák•ti va•om•ra ye•da•ber ado•ni ki chi•zak•tá•ni.

The Lord is good, a stronghold in the day of trouble; And He knows those who trust in Him.

Nahum 1:7

טוֹב יְהוָה לְמָעוֹז בְּיוֹם צָרָה וְיֹדֵעַ חֹסֵי בוֹ׃

Tov Adonái le•ma•oz be•yom tza•ra ve•yo•dé•a cho•séy vo.

Adonai Hoo Sha•lom – יְהוָה הוּא שָׁלוֹם

"THE LORD IS PEACE"

Come to Me, all who are weary and burdened, and I will give you rest. Take My yoke upon you and learn from Me, for I am gentle and humble in heart, and 'you will find rest for your souls.' For My yoke is easy and My burden is light."

Matthew 11:28-30 Tree of Life Bible

פְּנוּ-אֵלַי כָּל-עָמֵל וּמְסֻבָּל וַאֲנִי אֶתֵּן לָכֶם מַרְגּוֹעַ׃
שְׂאוּ אֶת-עֻלִּי עֲלֵיכֶם וְלִמְדוּ מִמֶּנִּי כִּי-עָנָיו אָנֹכִי וְשַׁח לֵבָב וְתִמְצְאוּ
מְנוּחָה לְנַפְשֹׁתֵיכֶם׃
כִּי עֻלִּי רַךְ וּמַשָּׂאִי קָל׃

P`nu-e•lai kol-amel oom•su•bal va•a•ni e•ten la•chem mar•go•a.
S`oo et-oo•li aley•chem ve•lim•du mi•me•ni ki-anav ano•chi ve•shach
le•vav ve•tim•tze•oo me•nu•cha le•naf•sho•tey•chem.
Ki oo•li rach oo•ma•sa•ee kal.

CONFESSING THE HEBREW SCRIPTURES

Adonai Hoo Sha•lom – יְהוָה הוּא שָׁלוֹם

"THE LORD IS PEACE"

... "Shalom I leave you, My shalom I give to you; but not as the world gives! Do not let your heart be troubled or afraid."

John 14:27 Tree of Life Bible

... שָׁלוֹם אֲנִי מַנִּיחַ לָכֶם אֶת-שְׁלוֹמִי אֲנִי נֹתֵן לָכֶם לֹא כַּאֲשֶׁר יִתֵּן הָעוֹלָם
אֲנִי נֹתֵן לָכֶם אַל-יִרְגַּז לִבְּכֶם וְאַל-יֵחָת:

... sha•lom ani ma•ni•ach la•chem et-sh`lo•mi ani no•ten la•chem lo cha•a•sher yi•ten ha•o•lam ani no•ten la•chem al-yir•gaz lib•chem ve•al-ye•chat.

Confessing the Hebrew Scriptures

Adonai Hoo Sha•lom – יְהוָה הוּא שָׁלוֹם

"THE LORD IS PEACE"

"These things I have spoken to you, so that in Me you may have shalom. In the world you will have trouble, but take heart! I have overcome the world!"

John 16:33 Tree of Life Bible

וַאֲנִי בַּדְּבָרִים הָאֵלֶּה בָּאתִי לְהַגִּיד לָכֶם כִּי בִי שָׁלוֹם יִהְיֶה-לָּכֶם בָּעוֹלָם
צָרָה תְּבוֹאַתְכֶם אַךְ-הִתְאַזְּרוּ עֹז אֲנִי נִצַּחְתִּי אֶת-הָעוֹלָם׃

Va•a•ni bad•va•rim ha•e•le ba•ti le•ha•gid la•chem ki vi sha•lom yi•hee•ye-la•chem ba•o•lam tza•ra t`vo•at•chem ach-hit•az•ru oz ani ni•tzach•ti et-ha•o•lam.

CONFESSING THE HEBREW SCRIPTURES

Adonai Hoo Sha•lom – יְהוָה הוּא שָׁלוֹם

"THE LORD IS PEACE"

Blessed be the God and Father of our Lord Yeshua the Messiah, the Father of compassion and God of all encouragement. He encourages us in every trouble, so that we may be able to encourage those who are in any trouble, through the very encouragement with which we ourselves are encouraged by God.

2 Corinthians 1:3-4 Tree of Life Bible

בָּרוּךְ הוּא הָאֱלֹהִים אֲבִי אֲדֹנֵינוּ יֵשׁוּעַ הַמָּשִׁיחַ אֲבִי הָרַחֲמִים וֵאלֹהֵי כָל-נֶחָמָה:
הַמְנַחֵם אֹתָנוּ בְּכָל-צָרָה וְהַנֹּתֵן לָנוּ כֹּחַ לְנַחֵם אֲחֵרִים בְּכָל-צָרָתָם
בְּתַנְחוּמִים אֲשֶׁר נֻחַמְנוּ מֵאֵת אֱלֹהִים:

Ba•ruch hoo ha•Elohim Avi Ado•ney•nu Yeshua ha•Ma•shi•ach Avi ha•ra•cha•mim ve•Elohey chol-ne•cha•ma.
Ha•me•na•chem o•ta•nu be•chol-tza•ra ve•ha•no•ten la•nu ko•ach le•na•chem a•che•rim be•chol-tza•ra•tam ba•tan•choo•mim asher nu•cham•nu me•et Elohim.

CONFESSING THE HEBREW SCRIPTURES

Adonai Hoo Sha•lom – יְהוָה הוּא שָׁלוֹם

"THE LORD IS PEACE"

... "My grace is sufficient for you, for power is made perfect in weakness." Therefore I will boast all the more gladly in my weaknesses, so that the power of Messiah may dwell in me. For Messiah's sake, then, I delight in weaknesses, in insults, in distresses, in persecutions, in calamities. For when I am weak, then I am strong.

2 Corinthians 12:9-10 Tree of Life Bible

... חַסְדִּי רַב-לְךָ כִּי לְאֵין אוֹנִים אַשְׁלִים גְּבוּרָתִי עַל-כֵּן מִטּוּב לֵב אֶתְהַלֵּל בְּתַחֲלוּאַי לְמַעַן תִּמָּצֵא בִי גְּבוּרַת הַמָּשִׁיחַ:
וְעַל-כֵּן רָצְתָה נַפְשִׁי בְּתַחֲלוּאִים וּבְגִדּוּפִים וְלִהְיוֹת נִרְדָּף וְלָשֶׁבֶת בְּמָצוֹק וּבְחֹסֶר כֹּל לְמַעַן הַמָּשִׁיחַ כִּי אִם-נְפוּגֹתִי אָז גִּבּוֹר אָנִי:

... chas•di rav-le•cha ki le•ein o•nim ash•lim g`vu•ra•ti al-ken mi•toov lev et•ha•lel be•ta•cha•lu•ai le•ma•an ti•ma•tze vi g`vu•rat ha•Ma•shi•ach. Ve•al-ken ratz•ta naf•shi ve•ta•cha•lu•eem oov•gi•doo•fim ve•li•hi•yot nir•daf ve•la•she•vet be•ma•tzok oov•cho•ser kol le•ma•an ha•Ma•shi•ach ki eem - n`fu•go•ti az gi•bor ani.

Confessing the Hebrew Scriptures

Adonai Hoo Sha•lom – יְהוָה הוּא שָׁלוֹם

"THE LORD IS PEACE"

...finally, brothers and sisters, rejoice! Aim for restoration, encourage one another, be of the same mind, live in shalom—and the God of love and shalom will be with you.

2 Corinthians 13:11 Tree of Life Bible

... הֱיוּ תְמִימִים וְהִתְחַזְּקוּ יַחְדּוּ אֶת־לִבְּכֶם וְאֶת־הַשָּׁלוֹם אֱהֶבוּ וֵאלֹהֵי הָאַהֲבָה וְהַשָּׁלוֹם יִהְיֶה עִמָּכֶם׃

... he•yu t`mi•mim ve•hit•cha•za•ku ya•cha•du et-lib•chem ve•et-ha•sha•lom e•he•vu ve•Elohey ha•a•ha•va ve•ha•sha•lom yi•hee•ye ee•ma•chem.

Confessing the Hebrew Scriptures

Adonai Hoo Sha•lom – יְהוָה הוּא שָׁלוֹם

"THE LORD IS PEACE"

Therefore, having been made righteous by trusting, we have shalom with God through our Lord Yeshua the Messiah. Through Him we also have gained access by faith into this grace in which we stand and boast in the hope of God's glory.

Romans 5:1-2 Tree of Life Bible

עַל-כֵּן כַּאֲשֶׁר נִצְדַּקְנוּ בָּאֱמוּנָה שָׁלוֹם יִשְׁפָּת-לָנוּ אֱלֹהִים עַל-יְדֵי יֵשׁוּעַ הַמָּשִׁיחַ אֲדֹנֵינוּ׃
אֲשֶׁר גַּם עַל-יָדוֹ מָצָאנוּ בְדֶרֶךְ אֱמוּנָה אֶת-שַׁעַר הַחֶסֶד אֲשֶׁר אֲנַחְנוּ בָאִים בּוֹ וּבְעֹז הָאֱלֹהִים נָרִים קֶרֶן כַּאֲשֶׁר קִוִּינוּ לוֹ׃

Al-ken ka•a•sher nitz•dak•nu va•e•mu•na sha•lom yish•pat-la•nu Elohim al-ye•dey Yeshua ha•Ma•shi•ach Ado•ney•nu.
Asher gam al-ya•do ma•tza•nu ve•de•rech e•mu•na et-sha•ar ha•che•sed asher a•nach•nu va•eem bo oov•oz ha•Elohim na•rim ke•ren ka•a•sher ki•vi•nu lo.

CONFESSING THE HEBREW SCRIPTURES

Adonai Hoo Sha•lom – יְהוָה הוּא שָׁלוֹם

"THE LORD IS PEACE"

For to be carnally minded is death, but to be spiritually minded is life and peace.

Romans 8:6

כִּי הֶגְיוֹן הַבָּשָׂר מָוֶת וְהֶגְיוֹן הָרוּחַ חַיִּים וְשָׁלוֹם׃

Ki heg•yon ha•ba•sar ma•vet ve•heg•yon ha•ru•ach cha•yim ve•sha•lom.

Now we know that all things work together for good for those who love God, who are called according to his purpose.

Romans 8:28 Tree of Life Bible

וְכָל־הַמַּעֲשִׂים יָדַעְנוּ כִּי יַעְזְרוּ יַחְדָּו לְטוֹבָה לְאֹהֲבֵי אֱלֹהִים הַקְּרֻאִים בְּסוֹד עֲצָתוֹ׃

Ve•chol-ha•ma•a•sim ya•da•a•nu ki ya•az•ru yach•dav le•to•va le•o•ha•vey Elohim hak•ru•eem be•sod a•tza•to.

Adonai Hoo Sha•lom – יְהוָה הוּא שָׁלוֹם

"THE LORD IS PEACE"

For I am convinced that neither death nor life, nor angels nor principalities, nor things present nor things to come, nor powers, nor height nor depth, nor any other created thing will be able to separate us from the love of God that is in Messiah Yeshua our Lord.

Romans 8:38-39 Tree of Life Bible

כִּי בָטַחְתִּי כִּי לֹא מָוֶת וְלֹא חַיִּים לֹא מַלְאֲכֵי אֵל לֹא שָׂרֵי הַצָּבָא לֹא
אֵלֶּה אֲשֶׁר יֶשְׁנָם וְלֹא אֵלֶּה אֲשֶׁר עֲתִדִים לָבֹא וְלֹא גִּבֹּרֵי כֹחַ:
וְלֹא רוּם וְלֹא עֹמֶק וְלֹא אֵיזֶה יְקוּם אַחֵר יִהְיֶה לְאֵל יָדָם לְהַפְרִידֵנוּ
מֵאַהֲבַת הָאֱלֹהִים אֲשֶׁר בְּיֵשׁוּעַ הַמָּשִׁיחַ אֲדֹנֵינוּ:

Ki va•tach•ti ki lo ma•vet ve•lo cha•yim lo mal•a•chey El lo sa•rey ha•tza•va lo ele asher yesh•nam ve•lo ele asher a•ti•dim la•vo ve•lo gi•bo•rey cho•ach.
Ve•lo room ve•lo o•mek ve•lo ey•ze ye•koom a•cher yi•hee•ye le•el ya•dam le•haf•ri•de•nu me•a•ha•vat ha•Elohim asher be•Yeshua ha•Ma•shi•ach Ado•ney•nu.

Adonai Hoo Sha•lom – יְהוָה הוּא שָׁלוֹם

"THE LORD IS PEACE"

For the kingdom of God is not about eating and drinking, but righteousness and shalom and joy in the Ruach ha-Kodesh.

Romans 14:17 Tree of Life Bible

כִּי-מַלְכוּת אֱלֹהִים אֵינֶנָּה מַאֲכָל וּמִשְׁתֶּה כִּי אִם-צְדָקָה שָׁלוֹם וְחֶדְוָה בְּרוּחַ הַקֹּדֶשׁ׃

Ki-mal•choot Elohim ey•ne•na ma•a•chal oo•mish•te ki eem-tze•da•ka sha•lom ve•ched•va be•Ru•ach ha•Ko•desh.

CONFESSING THE HEBREW SCRIPTURES

Adonai Hoo Sha•lom – יְהוָה הוּא שָׁלוֹם

"THE LORD IS PEACE"

Now may the God of hope fill you with all joy and shalom in trusting, so you may overflow with hope in the power of the Ruach ha-Kodesh.

Romans 15:13 Tree of Life Bible

וֵאלֹהֵי הַתִּקְוָה יְמַלֵּא אֶתְכֶם כָּל-שִׂמְחָה וְשָׁלוֹם בֶּאֱמוּנַתְכֶם לְהוֹסִיף חַיִל בְּתִקְוָה בְּעֹז רוּחַ הַקֹּדֶשׁ׃

Ve•Elohey ha•tik•va ye•ma•le et•chem kol-sim•cha ve•sha•lom be•e•mu•nat•chem le•ho•sif cha•yil be•tik•va be•oz Ru•ach ha•Ko•desh.

CONFESSING THE HEBREW SCRIPTURES

Adonai Hoo Sha•lom – יְהוָה הוּא שָׁלוֹם

"THE LORD IS PEACE"

Now the God of shalom will soon crush satan under your feet. May the grace of our Lord Yeshua be with you.

Romans 16:20 Tree of Life Bible

וֵאלֹהֵי הַשָּׁלוֹם יְדַכֵּא אֶת-הַשָּׂטָן כֹּה מַהֵר תַּחַת רַגְלֵיכֶם חֶסֶד יֵשׁוּעַ הַמָּשִׁיחַ
אֲדֹנֵינוּ יִהְיֶה עִמָּכֶם אָמֵן׃

Ve•Elohey ha•sha•lom ye•da•ke et-ha•Satan ko ma•her ta•chat rag•ley•chem che•sed Yeshua ha•Ma•shi•ach Ado•ney•nu yi•hee•ye ee•ma•chem Amen.

CONFESSING THE HEBREW SCRIPTURES

Adonai Hoo Sha•lom – יְהוָה הוּא שָׁלוֹם

"THE LORD IS PEACE"

Do not be anxious about anything—but in everything, by prayer and petition with thanksgiving, let your requests be made known to God. And the shalom of God, which surpasses all understanding, will guard your hearts and your minds in Messiah Yeshua.

Philippians 4:6 Tree of Life Bible

הַרְחִיקוּ כָּל-דְּאָגָה מִכֶּם אַךְ הוֹדִיעוּ כָּל-מִשְׁאֲלוֹתֵיכֶם בִּתְפִלָּה בִּתְחִנָּה
וּבְתוֹדָה לֵאלֹהֵינוּ׃
וְהָאֱלֹהִים יְצַו אֶת-שְׁלוֹמוֹ אֲשֶׁר לֹא יְכִילֶנּוּ כָּל-שֵׂכֶל לִנְצֹר אֶת-לִבְּכֶם
וְאֶת-הֶגְיוֹן רוּחֲכֶם בְּיֵשׁוּעַ הַמָּשִׁיחַ׃

Har•chi•ku chol-de•a•ga mi•kem ach ho•di•oo chol-mish•alo•tey•chem bit•fi•la bit•chi•na oov•to•da le•Elohey•nu.
Ve•ha•Elohim ye•tzav et-Sh`lo•mo asher lo ye•chi•le•nu chol-se•chel lin•tzor et-lib•chem ve•et-heg•yon ru•cha•chem be•Yeshua ha•Ma•shi•ach.

CONFESSING THE HEBREW SCRIPTURES

Adonai Hoo Sha•lom – יְהוָה הוּא שָׁלוֹם

"THE LORD IS PEACE"

And in Him you have been filled to fullness. He is the head over every ruler and authority.

Colossians 2:10 Tree of Life Bible

וְאַתֶּם מְמֻלָּאִים בּוֹ אֲשֶׁר הוּא הָרֹאשׁ לְכָל-מִשְׂרָה וְשִׁלְטוֹן׃

Ve•a•tem me•mu•la•eem bo asher hoo ha•rosh le•chol-mis•ra ve•shil•ton.

Let the shalom of Messiah rule in your hearts—to this shalom you were surely called in one body. Also be thankful.

Colossians 3:15 Tree of Life Bible

וּשְׁלוֹם הָאֱלֹהִים אֲשֶׁר-נִבְחַרְתֶּם לוֹ בְּגוּף אֶחָד יִמְשֹׁל בְּקֶרֶב לִבְּכֶם
וְאֶת-טוּבוֹ תַּכִּירוּ׃

Oosh•lom ha•Elohim asher-niv•char•tem lo be•goof e•chad yim•shol be•ke•rev lib•chem ve•et-too•vo ta•ki•ru.

Confessing the Hebrew Scriptures

Adonai Hoo Sha•lom – יְהוָה הוּא שָׁלוֹם

"THE LORD IS PEACE"

Now may the God of shalom Himself make you completely holy; and may your whole spirit and soul and body be kept complete, blameless at the coming of our Lord Yeshua the Messiah. Faithful is the One who calls you—and He will make it happen!

1 Thessalonians 5:23-24 Tree of Life Bible

וֵאלֹהֵי הַשָּׁלוֹם הוּא יְקַדֵּשׁ אֶתְכֶם מֵהָחֵל וְעַד-כַּלֵּה וְיִשְׁמָרְכֶם מִכָּל-רָע
בְּרוּחַ נֶפֶשׁ וּגְוִיָּה לְמוֹעֵד בּוֹא אֲדֹנֵינוּ יֵשׁוּעַ הַמָּשִׁיחַ׃
נֶאֱמָן הוּא הַקֹּרֵא אֶתְכֶם וְהוּא גַּם-יַעֲשֶׂה׃

Ve•Elohey ha•sha•lom hoo ye•ka•desh et•chem me•ha•chel ve•ad-ka•le ve•yish•mor•chem mi•kol-ra be•ru•ach ne•fesh oog•vi•ya le•mo•ed bo Ado•ney•nu Yeshua ha•Ma•shi•ach.
Ne•e•man hoo ha•ko•re et•chem ve•hoo gam-ya•a•se.

Confessing the Hebrew Scriptures

Adonai Hoo Sha•lom – יְהוָה הוּא שָׁלוֹם

"THE LORD IS PEACE"

Now may the Lord of shalom Himself give you shalom at all times and in every way. The Lord be with you all!

2 Thessalonians 3:16 Tree of Life Bible

וַאֲדוֹן הַשָּׁלוֹם הוּא יִתֵּן לָכֶם שָׁלוֹם בְּכֹל אֲשֶׁר תִּפְנוּ כָּל-הַיָּמִים וַאֲדֹנֵינוּ יְהִי עִם-כֻּלְּכֶם׃

Va•Adon ha•sha•lom hoo yi•ten la•chem sha•lom be•chol asher tif•noo kol-ha•ya•mim va•Ado•ney•nu ye•hee eem-kool•chem.

For God has not given us a spirit of timidity but of power and love and self-discipline.

2 Timothy 1:7 Tree of Life Bible

כִּי לֹא נָתַן לָנוּ אֱלֹהִים רוּחַ פָּחַד כִּי אִם-רוּחַ גְּבוּרָה אַהֲבָה וּמוּסָר׃

Ki lo na•tan la•nu Elohim ru•ach pa•chad ki eem-ru•ach g`vu•ra a•ha•va oo•mu•sar.

Adonai Hoo Sha•lom – יְהוָה הוּא שָׁלוֹם

"THE LORD IS PEACE"

So there remains a Shabbat rest for the people of God. For the one who has entered God's rest has also ceased from his own work, just as God did from His.

Hebrews 4:9-10 Tree of Life Bible

וְלָכֵן עוֹד נִשְׁאַר יוֹם שַׁבָּתוֹן לְעַם אֱלֹהִים׃
כִּי הַבָּא אֶל-מְנוּחָתוֹ יִשְׁבֹּת מִמְּלַאכְתּוֹ כַּאֲשֶׁר גַּם-שָׁבַת אֱלֹהִים מִמְּלַאכְתּוֹ שֶׁלּוֹ׃

Ve•la•chen od nish•ar yom sha•ba•ton le•am Elohim.
Ki ha•ba el-me•nu•cha•to yish•bot mim•lach•to ka•a•sher gam - sha•vat Elohim mim•lach•to she•lo.

CONFESSING THE HEBREW SCRIPTURES

Adonai Hoo Sha•lom – יְהוָה הוּא שָׁלוֹם

"THE LORD IS PEACE"

... "I will never leave you or forsake you," so that with confidence we say, "The Lord is my helper; I will not fear. What will man do to me?"

Hebrews 13:5-6 Tree of Life Bible

...לֹא אַרְפְּךָ וְלֹא אֶעֱזְבֶךָ׃
עַל-כֵּן נִבְטַח וְנֹאמַר יְהוָֹה לִי בְּעֹזְרִי לֹא אִירָא מַה-יַּעֲשֶׂה לִי אָדָם׃

... lo ar•pe•cha ve•lo e•ez•ve•cha.
Al-ken niv•tach ve•no•mar Adonai li be•oz•rai lo ee•ra ma-ya•a•se li adam.

Confessing the Hebrew Scriptures

Adonai Hoo Sha•lom – יְהוָה הוּא שָׁלוֹם

"THE LORD IS PEACE"

And let endurance have its perfect work, so that you may be perfect and complete, lacking in nothing.

Jacob 1:4 Tree of Life Bible

וּפְעֻלַּת כֹּחַ הַסַּבָּל תִּהְיֶה שְׁלֵמָה לְבַעֲבוּר תִּהְיוּ שְׁלֵמִים וּתְמִימִים וְלֹא יֶחְסַר לָכֶם דָּבָר׃

Oof•oo•lat ko•ach ha•sa•bal ti•hi•ye sh`le•ma le•va•a•voor ti•hi•yu sh`le•mim oot•mi•mim ve•lo yech•sar la•chem da•var.

CONFESSING THE HEBREW SCRIPTURES

Adonai Hoo Sha•lom – יְהוָה הוּא שָׁלוֹם

"THE LORD IS PEACE"

But the wisdom that is from above is first pure, then peaceable, gentle, open to reason, full of mercy and good fruits, impartial, not hypocritical. And the fruit of righteousness is sown in shalom by those who make shalom.

Jacob 3:17-18 Tree of Life Bible

אַךְ הַחָכְמָה הַיֹּרֶדֶת מֵעָל טְהוֹרָה הִיא פִּיהָ תִּפְתַּח לְשָׁלוֹם וּבַעֲנָוָה דְּבָרֶיהָ נוֹחָה הִיא לְהִתְרַצּוֹת מְלֵאָה רַחֲמִים וּפִרְיָהּ טוֹב אֵין עִמָּהּ מַשֹּׂא פָנִים וְאֵין חֲנֻפָּה בָּהּ:

זֶה פְּרִי הַצְּדָקָה זָרֻעַ לָבֶטַח לְעֹשֵׂי שָׁלוֹם:

Ach ha•choch•ma ha•yo•re•det me•al te•ho•ra hee pi•ha tif•tach le•sha•lom oo•va•ana•va d`va•re•ha no•cha hee le•hit•ra•tzot me•le•ah ra•cha•mim oo•fir•ya tov eyn ee•ma ma•so fa•nim ve•eyn cha•nu•pa ba.
Ze p`ri ha•tz`da•ka za•ru•a la•ve•tach le•o•sey sha•lom.

CONFESSING THE HEBREW SCRIPTURES

Adonai Hoo Sha•lom – יְהוָה הוּא שָׁלוֹם

"THE LORD IS PEACE"

May grace and shalom be multiplied to you in the knowledge of God and of Yeshua our Lord. His divine power has given us everything we need for life and godliness, through the knowledge of Him who called us by His own glory and virtue.

2 Peter 1:2-3 Tree of Life Bible

חֶסֶד לָכֶם וְשָׁלוֹם רָב בְּדַעַת אֱלֹהִים וְיֵשׁוּעַ אֲדֹנֵינוּ׃
כַּאֲשֶׁר נָתַן לָנוּ יְהוָה בִּגְבוּרָתוֹ כָּל-מִשְׁעַן הַחַיִּים וְיִרְאַת שָׁמָיִם עַל-יְדֵי דַעַת הַקֹּרֵא אֹתָנוּ בְּעֹז צִדְקָתוֹ׃

Che•sed la•chem ve•sha•lom rav be•da•at Elohim ve•Yeshua Ado•ney•nu. Ka•a•sher na•tan la•nu Adonai big•vu•ra•to kol-mish•an ha•cha•yim ve•yir•at sha•ma•yim al-ye•dey da•at ha•ko•re o•ta•nu be•oz tzid•ka•to.